the widow's coat

miriam sagan

ahsahta press

Boise State University • Boise, Idaho • 2002

Ahsahta Press, Boise State University
Boise, Idaho 83725
http://ahsahtapress.boisestate.edu

Copyright © 1999 by Miriam Sagan

Printed in the United States of America
Cover photograph by Lenny Foster
Second printing 2002
ISBN 0-916272-67-2

Library of Congress Catalog Card Number
98-74926

contents

Note: A centered asterisk at the foot of a recto page of poetry indicates that the poem continues over to the next page.

acknowledgments

Some of these poems first appeared in *Are We There Yet, Blue Mesa Review, The Connecticut Review, The New Mexican, Nimrod, The XY Files* (Sherman Asher Publishing), *Another Desert: The Jewish Poetry of New Mexico* (Sherman Asher, 1998), and *Rio* (online).

author's introduction

These poems were written during an intense period, starting shortly before my husband's death and taking about twenty months to complete. My husband Robert Winson was a Zen priest, ordained in the Japanese Soto lineage. He worked in Santa Fe's main library, had a punk band called Bichos, and a literary magazine, *Fish Drum*. At the age of thirty-four, he fell seriously ill from the effects of ulcerative colitis. We had been married for thirteen years when Robert died from the aftereffects of surgery. I was forty-one. He was thirty-six. Our daughter was six. At first I could not write at all, which should have been no surprise, as I couldn't walk or eat or sleep either. But after a few months passed, writing poetry became, if not exactly therapeutic, a natural way to deal with an outpouring of feeling.

People assumed that because I was a poet it would be easy and natural for me to write about these events, but it was not. After Robert's death, poetry seemed insignificant. But still, out of some unconscious mechanism, I wrote. This is the document of that experience.

Part of what fueled the poems is the fact that after I was widowed I fell in love again. This was as startling to me as to those around me, because in some primitive way I believed that my life was now over. However, I turned out to be wrong. I fell in love with the man who had been my high school boyfriend, and a friend ever since. Perhaps no one ever falls completely out of love—and ours had been dormant. He came two thousand miles to pay a condolence call. When we became reinvolved after twenty-three years apart I began to write even more. A tumultuous conjunction of grief and love was the nexus for many of these poems. Old memories were awakened, and became poetic sources.

There is something slightly shocking about the mixture of love and death. I learned from experience and observation that those who were happily married tend to marry again—widowhood is less disillusioning than divorce. But even in contemporary society a widow may feel herself somehow taboo—not allowed to truly live. These primitive experiences are also part of the poetry, for although we may forget it, poetry itself can and should be startling.

These poems are set in the Southwest region that I live in and love—from the ruins of Pecos Pueblo to my own small house on Santa Fe's unfashionable west side. They range over interior landscapes, borders, myth, and memory.

My greatest appreciation is due to Carol Moldaw for her help with this manuscript, as both friend and poet.

Miriam Sagan
Santa Fe, New Mexico

crematorium

I saw you, literally, go up in smoke
From the parking lot on Luisa Street
Italian mortuary in a Spanish town
Heat waves turned the air
A malleable screen
This is what I saw, husband
Against force field your body made a fuel
$E=mc^2$; I saw
A tree, lines of telephone wires
Like a black score
It was October
There might have been some common birds
My face above your Chinese coat
Was something out of a Russian poem
Akhmatova in Turkestan
Some displaced person, a woman
Who was not
Where she had planned to stand.

Inside the mortuary was a hush
Of catholicism and dim light
A headstone for a child
Your corpse lay perfectly cold
In a drawer next to "Baby Ortega"
My friend said that when she heard
Someone sobbing in the ladies' room
She thought it was a friend of ours
When a stranger came out the door
She suddenly remembered
Other people were suffering too.
I move backwards in time

*

Your corpse becomes a coma
I'm holding first your hands, then your feet
Cold without oxygen
Wrapped in a body temperature blanket
Of plastic
Your eyes must have been bandaged
Someone emptied a bucket of blood
I'm moving backwards
In the black and white photo my brother took
You are twenty-two, bearded, standing by city beach
At the ruined Sutro Baths.

Dead, a priest I don't know
Japanese lineage, shaves you
With the razor a friend thought to bring
This second ordination
Prepares you for a white kimono of flames
Prepares me for nothing
Not what I'll tell your daughter
Not whose mouth I'll kiss
Not if I'll ever look at the ocean again.

I tell myself I'll give up
What I no longer desire:
Mozart, Patti Smith,
Jewelry, sleep, prayer, rectitude
I'll acquire
Land in a state you didn't like
Tickets to where no English is spoken
A black cat named Orpheo
That is a warning
Black Orpheus who looks back

Down the winding stair to hell
Gets torn to pieces later in the story
Love, I won't look back
You're gone, you're ash
I hold this grief
Built to outlast you.

what my friends think

My friends think what women think
They think you are very sick but you will not die
They think: men move furniture, men make money
Men make love to you, you can blame them.
These are the main things men are good for.
Men can give you jewelry, they can give you herpes
They can make you cry.
They can take you to dinner, they can marry you
You can blame them. Men die.
My friends think someday they will be alone
Any woman can live in a world without men
But not in a world without women.
My friends think a sick husband is like any husband
A sick husband does not wash dishes, buy you jewelry, or paint the trim
Nor does a well husband.
My friends think women are human and men are mammals.
Women invented pottery, agriculture, singing, weaving, and lunch.
Men invented war and French kissing.
My friends think it is best to eat with women
In the day time
And men at night.
My friends think you are sick but do not care
As much as if you were their husband.
My friends think all husbands are sick—
They smoke cigarettes, crack up the car, flirt
They snort heroin, they have
Heart attacks, strokes, senility.
Who can tell what they feel or if they suffer as we do.
They are men.

my husband

My husband in stubble, zen priest in a nicotine patch
My husband by the open grave with a handful of dirt
My husband the Jew, bleeding from ulcers
My husband in ivory beads carved into skulls
A man with designer sunglasses, speeding tickets, the collected works of
        Han Shan
Of weight loss, skinny as Auschwitz, whose new name is colitis
Whose other name means water course in Japanese
Whose name was taken from the western sycamore tree
Whose original name was changed on Ellis Island
Who began to vomit the day I kissed him
My husband who buys one pair of boots per lifetime
Who loses forty pounds, whose wrists
Make me hysterical, who molts, parakeet or polar bear
My husband who swam without his glasses
Towards a horizon marked by a red tanker
Who stood up and hemorrhaged rust
Who wrote his initials in blood
Who coached me in childbirth
Who owed me fifty dollars
Who gave me a mushroom
Who moves the sprinklers
Who cut up the counter with a carving knife
Who crossed his legs and sat down
Whose name was raven and anemia and something else secret
An internal organ shaped like Minnesota
Shadow, skeleton, moth owl
Sitting on a cache of eggs in the dark
City sitting on its own skyline
Empire State Building, Arc de Triomphe, Coit Tower
This curve of the world lit up by expensive
Electricity I call husband.

oryoki

Standing barefoot
On the parquet floorboards
Of my mother's house
My mouth formed the word:
Shalako
All night Zuñi ceremony
I've never been to
Her brother is there
Two thousand miles and more to the west
Something is making a dry sound
A bed of brittle twigs
Beneath New York City

Last night in the dream
Things were very bad
You'd been shot, trying
To protect us from a black dog
You were dead in the dream
And I could see your ghost
Smiling faintly
Packing up in the calm manner
Of a priest going to a monastery
You folded the little cloths
For your oryoki bowls
You were planning to eat
Three bowls of rice
In the land of the dead.
Sweetheart, your expression
Didn't inspire me with confidence—
You seemed too pleased
To go.

he dreams

Alive, he dreams of Key West
Alley behind the Cuban bakery
Strip of palms screening a shack
A good feeling of anticipation
Like turning over a rock and finding a turtle.
Alive, he dreams of a basement
Full of tanks of fish
He has neglected to feed
The tanks are overgrown
Fish shine like neon
In the window of a cocktail lounge.

Dead, he dreams of me
He dreams I am standing in the kitchen
In a white nightgown he has never seen
I am holding a vegetable cleaver
That has been improperly sharpened
Attempting to cut a blood orange into quarters.
In the dream he wants to yell:
Use a different knife
Do you know how many people I've seen
Cut themselves that way?

Dead, he dreams about the proper equipment:
A bag for the binoculars,
The best snow shovel,
A good pen, an extension cord,
A tiny microphone, an electric bass.
Dead, I dream of him
Back in the house,
Angry that I've given everything away.

*

Alive, he dreamed his body
Was being cut up and thrown into the sea.
Alive, he dreamed of Key West
Of an ocean
Where any flesh was bait for the unexpected.

translation from a dead language

My mother-in-law gave me a knife
To open letters
Don't ask me
From whom
It was ominous, and black,
Blade of stone, or bone

Later, she confessed
She knew it was bad luck
To give a knife
Asked for two pennies
Like the kind we placed on your eyes for fare
So she could sell it back to me.

Really, this isn't the worst
Thing that can happen to a widow
The neighbors poured kerosene
On a girl
Who'd borne sons to their son
And lit a kitchen match—
I understand
No family can bear
A widow's eyes—
The look of grief
Or of something quite different.

i know who you are

Last night I dreamed that you weren't dead
We'd broken up
You were still sick, but well enough
To hold a job.
I yelled at you on the phone: why the hell
Can't you come home once in a while
And read your daughter a good night story?

You are a 36-year-old ghost—
You will never be any older
In the photograph your head is shaved, zen priest
You wear a red T-shirt, you smile
You hold a doll's head
Which you are repairing
You haven't looked this good in years.

You are my first husband.
You are my husband
You are a four-month-old dead person
Like a four-month-old fetus
No one can feel you move
I might still abort or miscarry you,
Like a developing baby
With each month you become increasingly
Dead.

Now you are a reason—
The reason your sister will not get out of bed,
The reason your other sister has a migraine
The reason acquaintances embrace me
My friends enquire of each other: how is she?
The reason a man who is not you

Tells me on the phone: I love you
Passionately
You are the reason I won't listen
To Otis Redding
The reason N. has a flashback, A. hates her husband,
L. weeps, that my phone bill is $500.

I know who you were:
Near-sighted, hilarious,
Bad-tempered, a terrible driver,
The only person I'll ever know
Who read Shakespeare in a dull moment for pleasure
I know who you are: ash, bone,
A name, my tears,
Mail that arrives
That cannot be properly delivered
Nor properly returned.

handwriting

I see rain fall on the end of summer
Yellow chamisa and the orange leaves
Of my neighbor Grace's apricot tree
I see rain smear color like memory,
Color draining out of the world
Like New York City rainbow oilslick
Vanishing down the sewer grate.

Your handwriting is still everywhere in my house
You had beautiful handwriting, clear and bold,
And it has outlasted you.
I keep the bits and pieces
I couldn't bear to throw away.
Your calendar where the last thing written
Is "surgery"
And then the rest is blank.
The mail arrives for me, for my child,
For you, for the couple who lived here,
For Angel who doesn't live here,
Mail arrives for the dead and the living.
I should take your name off the gas bill,
I should take your name off the electric bill.

I read your notebooks without fear of revelation.
After all, years ago,
You burned those love letters from Miss X
In a tin can in the front yard of the old apartment.
I don't see your ghost on the corner
The way your friends and sisters can
To be honest, I don't want you around
You're dead, I'm not, we have to break up
As surely as if you'd run off to Cleveland with Miss X.

I believe I will be happy.
I am the only widow in my family
But I am not the most unhappy person.
I believe I will paint the bedroom pink
I will go to Hawaii, and to Trinidad, Colorado
I will buy red velvet to wear all winter.
Since you died I have danced at a wedding,
Been on three boats, seen falling stars
And been given a free papaya at the market.
I believe I will live to be old without you.

I see your handwriting
On the words of the Buddhist gatha
On the note saying: "Mir,
Let's Have A Date."
I see your coat in the closet
I see your eyelashes on your daughter
Your smile in her smile
I see her sob, and hit the pillow,
Wailing for you.
I'm glad I don't see you as a ghost,
Thank you for not coming back.
The last time I saw you in a dream
You were lying in the bathtub
With your abdomen patched in black rubber.
You said: "Tomorrow I'll be dead."
I'd like to see you well in a dream.
I see rain falling over New Mexico.
I say: good-bye, I'll see you later.

grief

The Polynesians have one word that means
You feel the canoe rocking
As you rocked all day
Even though you lie in your bed at night

In English there is a word
I can't remember
For when it rains twenty thousand feet in the air
To ten thousand, then stops,
Rain never hitting the ground

The letter from the dead painter
To you, also dead, falls out
Of a book I am reading to our daughter
He hopes you are swimming at the beach
That he will leave the v.a. hospital to paint

You never swam again
The envelope is blank
Everything I see has outlasted you
The language of grief.

mountain peak grave

Plant a corkscrew willow
On your grave—
I'd rather leave my bra
After all, you loved women
Even more than trees.

I'm just a laywoman
We don't mean the same thing
The calligraphy in translation reads
Existence and non-existence
Are the same.

Monks of this mountain monastery
You eat cold soup
From a cold bowl
When will you depart
And start following the way?

mythology

The strangers who appear at the door
Might be looking
For the neighbor's auto repair lot
Might be Girl Scouts
Selling cookies
Or Jehovah's Witnesses
Passing out tracts
Greet them politely
The strangers who appear
Might be gods, tired and hungry.

Two gods in disguise
Must grant a favor
To the husband and wife
Who fed them flat bread and olives
All these mortal lovers ask
Is to die together
So that one
Must not stand
By the other's grave.

I wasn't home
When these gods came to call
So you and I
Did not turn into trees together
Did not have arms
Turn into branches
Bark cover our faces
Did not wave forever
Green in the wind
I've had my luck
Some call good, some

Call otherwise
Had houseguests and stray cats
For a lifetime of dinners
But did not get my wish
One wish only
No strangers or angels
Knock unexpectedly.

forest fire

Stone lions
Ringed by fire
The wilderness burns
Dome of the Jemez Mountains
Caldera you can see from the moon
When the highest mountain on earth
Blew its top. Stone Buddha
Reclining in Parinirvana, death.
You lay very still
In the coma
But your sister says
She saw you crying
I'd told you not to die
Until she got there.
You've missed the biggest
Forest fire in twenty years
Ash from forty miles away
Fell on my student Rose's head
Smoke drifted
Through the potted pansies
The sun went dark
The night glowed like an ember
At the end of a cigarette
Midnights you'd sit
Not wanting company
On the front porch, unable
To sleep, watching
The empty street.

birthday of the dead

Because you are dead
You won't see
Two white Siberian tigers
Asleep in the Albuquerque sun
Or the scarlet ibis
Red as Egypt in flames
Or me in a black silk nightgown

Because you are dead
You won't take off this nightgown
Or object
When another lover strokes my breasts
You won't open the window to smell
Smoke of the forest fire
Worst in thirty years
As the Jemez Dome burns
Because you are dead
You won't rush to the front porch
To see that smoke black out the sun
Sun red as the scarlet ibis
Or the blood I draw up
With two fingers from between my legs

Because you are dead
On this Sunday, your birthday
You do not turn 37
You remain 36
Someone else had my virginity
Holds my breasts
Because you are dead.

angel

I saw an angel on the cargo ferry
Going back to the mainland
In the opposite direction of mine.
You'd been dead over nine months
By high summer, and grief
Moved into term from gestation.
I was coming back to the island that evening
In a light misty rain
As *The Islander* docked
In Vineyard Haven
I glanced across the Sunday night crowd
To find an angel among them.
The angel was seven feet, tall as a Gothic spire,
A white robe with wings folded
Facing away from the open water
Sitting where no passengers were allowed
On the deck of the vehicles only ferry.

Why was an angel
Leaving the island?
Going back to the city, to work, to Monday
As if the angel had been on vacation.
Every night after you died
Our daughter asked me if I'd seen an angel
She saw them crowded thick in the room like moths
One that looked like you standing on a telephone wire.

"All you have to do is believe," she'd say
She was so happy when I told her my secret
"See any more you-know-whats?" she'd ask.
Now the season has turned towards winter
I've left the island

With its deer and goldenrod
Its hightide of beach plums
Where wind cuts like a razor clam.
Summer is gone, the placenta
That nourished you—ghost—
Is withering
You can't be born
Nor can you die again.
My daughter says she no longer
Sees angels
She told me: "The angels
Are gone
Because we are better
But they'll come if we need them:
The Angel of Hope
The Angel of Change."

late august

If I didn't know
What I know
I'd think this could go on
Indefinitely
Painting the bookshelves pink
The legs of the table blue
Under a summer sky
Or later in the day
A party in the shade
Little girls weaving crowns
Of ribbon and gold wire.
No guest minds
That the new house
Is really an old house
Decrepit around the edges
Of the yard where the acequia runs.
The still young woman
About to have her third child
Has arranged her peacock earrings
Around the rim of a drinking glass.
Chinese elms
Drip some sap
On the birthday party
Where my daughter has changed
Into the birthday girl's satin nightgown.
If I didn't know
What I know too well
The smell of roasting chilis
In the air
Wouldn't signal something.
Indian Market
Has packed up its turquoise stones and rain.
If there is one thing I know for certain—
I will never see you again.

a new autobiography

Things change—you throw a stone in the pond
Freeze frame on a ripple
Call that ripple "my life"—my marriage, my house, my child
From a star in the Andromeda galaxy
That ripple barely exists
Pond is too small to see
Let alone the stone in your palm.

When I was fifteen
I kissed a boy on the mouth
It was July.
This was not the first boy I had ever kissed
I opened my mouth just a little
At fifteen I called lust research, curiosity, danger, not pleasure yet.
I was the first girl
This boy had ever kissed.

Like Tristan and Isolde
In *La Morte D'Arthur*
I was carrying a love potion in a bottle
I was on a boat to meet a king
But instead I poured the charm
Into the young knight's cup of wine
We drank it down.
We kissed.
I left when I was almost nineteen.
If I dreamed of him
It was only to see him in an overcoat in the rain.

I moved from city to city
I got married, bought a stucco house

*

On the west side, had a daughter
My husband fell sick
Our daughter grew, she toddled, walked
I made money, and I spent it too
The mail arrived, my husband
Lay in bed, I drove
Him to tests, to doctor waits,
Sparrows nested in the eaves

Our daughter grew, she talked, blew bubbles
She asked: "Is Dad going to die?"
He grew thin, shrank,
Beneath a surgeon's knife—he died.
People crammed the house, I was forty-two
I was hysterical, I was a widow
I said Kaddish, I wept, I went to the grocery store
I bought four snow tires
I received condolence calls.
The boy I'd kissed
Came to visit
He arrived by airplane at night
His hair was grey
He had sworn off women
His heart was broken.
He said: "I knew
I could never resist you."

point hope

After you died
I began traveling by dog sled
Day and night...

I went out to trap a seal early in the morning
When I came back, my husband was dead
His body lay half in and half out of the shack
Burned by the kerosene heater, frozen in the snow
Dogs whined on the line
Tied to the stump of a tree that had no reason to be there
I took my knife and shaved his face bare
But I couldn't move the body alone
There was no fuel. The tundra was frozen.
I couldn't slip the gold wedding band off his finger.
I put the seal carcass on the sled and hitched up the dogs.

When the Bering Strait is frozen
You can cross it, from island to island
I drove the dogs, and they ran
Southeast across a frozen sea.
Aurora Borealis played both day and night
Echoing green as a bass drum in my ear.
I ate the seal, piece by cold piece, fed the dogs
Who hated me.
In this fashion I traveled from the Arctic Circle
Until January, when I reached
The small decrepit town of Point Hope.

It was a town of mud streets, a bar,
Tarpaper windows, a frozen bay
The hundred or so inhabitants of the town

*

Looked shocked to see me on my sled
I cut the lines and set the dogs free
Then fainted on the icy street.
I came to in a bed beneath a skin
In a room lit by fire
"I am the mayor of Point Hope"
Said a voice as a man's face
Came into focus above my pain.

antelope season

We arrived at night
Driving in rain across the pass
From Raton, New Mexico to Trinidad, Colorado
The street was empty, dark hilly neighborhood
That spoke of mines
Opening and closing,
A drop in the price of silver.
Temple Aaron on erev Rosh Hashanah
Stone synagogue, built in 1883
With a red wooden cupola
Perched on its roof
Like a rakish hat on a plump lady.

Entering the shul
My eyes flooded with tears,
That smell—incense, furniture polish, wax, desire,
Despair, hope, prayers of childbirth, and cancer,
Bankruptcy, new love, and lost land.
We sat on velvet cushions
In a congregation of only thirty
We could not have felt more far-away
In Shanghai, or Lima.
We were the only Jews
Between Denver and El Paso.

Stained glass windows
Reached from floor to ceiling
An abstract pattern of blue and orange.
My daughter pressed her nose against a pane
Inside each colored square
A mysterious fire was dancing

*

Double helix glittering and moving
I could find no source
To that trick of light
That kept dancing.
I recited the prayer for the dead, my dead,
That puzzling prayer, Kaddish,
Which offers no consolation

But the praise of God.
Yellow lines of the highway led me here.
Redwing blackbirds flocked
Antelopes grazed
By the side of the road among sunflowers and chamisa.
It was antelope season in these days
Of awe when the hinge swings
Between earth and heaven
Days that run quickly
Hooves pounding
The dust of plains we call home.

canyon el grande

Why would a one-armed man
Take a wooden boat
Down the rapids
Of this violent, bejeweled river?

A year after your death
I read the journals
Of John Wesley Powell
Even this explorer
Had a boat named for his wife

At Separation Rapids
Three of his men left him
To climb to the rim
Less afraid of the unknown
Than of white water—
Never seen again.

Anxiety, an enclosed horizon
Unable for days
To see 360 degrees of sky.

To exit
And find a group of unknown fishermen
Dredging for your corpse.

I followed the river once,
In the hotel in Gallup
Waiting for the train
Scoured by river sand
I knew I'd never be the same—

"Above, it is a chasm;
Below, it is a stairway
From gloom to heaven"
From past to present
A ladder with rungs of light.

a widow's kaddish

Standing behind the screen
Listening to the minyan of men
I stand up and say Kaddish
For my dead husband
That ladder of prayer
Aramaic with rungs of Hebrew

A prayer like smoke
Or a well-worn pathway
Ancient Polynesian trail on the Na Pali Coast
Stones worn smooth by passing feet
Or handholds in Frijoles Canyon
Scooped from tuff to the mesa top

Lines on the palm—
Lines on the map—
Neither prepared me for the terrain itself
Lifeline ends
Luminous monitor goes flat
Your heart fails
The weeping nurse
Disconnects you
From respirator that fills your lungs
With artificial air.

Arm of the starfish
Leg of the salamander
Neural pathway
That can rejuvenate
I'll drink a shot of schnapps
L'Chaim—
It's late at night
We're getting a little drunk
Jupiter is hanging
Brilliant object above the shul's parking lot
I go home singing
In the dark.

day of the dead

I wanted to buy
Skeletons, sugar skulls, at the little shop
A skeleton of a lute-playing mermaid
Spiney as a fish
Or the skeleton of a writer
Sitting with tits, leg-crossed
Smoking a cigarette
Death's black typewriter
With an inky message in Spanish

Still, the bones were overpriced
Tourist prices for the plaza
We moved from years ago
Besides, it frightened me
The skeleton bride and groom
On the top of the cake
Last month at the wedding
And the casual way
The groom gestured
To a Balinese shroud
Decorating one of his cottonwood trees

I went instead
Into the Japanese store
You used to like
And was shocked at how expensive
The iron teapot was
You'd bought years ago.
Do I expect to see you
On this unexpectedly blue and balmy day in November?
I expect so.
I expect not.

at the border

I am a widow in Juárez
As I am in El Paso, Texas—
But south of the Rio Grande
Facades are green and lavender,
The pink wall of the Shangri La
Chinese restaurant
Runs like a dream of color across the eye.
Women out of the Sierra Madres
Are begging with styrofoam cups
We sit at metal tables
Drinking Coca-Cola
And buy five tiny fabric dolls
From a little girl in braids.
My daughter gives quarters and pennies
To anyone who asks her.
The river is damned, impassable
The notion of border
Between one world and the next
Seems ridiculous, impossible
As if the dead didn't visit us,
Ghosts of Texas and ghosts of Juárez.
From the north you can see Mexico
A series of pastel squares
Startling on one of the houses
A Star of David outlined in light bulbs.
The trolley runs across, as does desire, does air
The two sides of the coin
Wanting each other's shadow.
The face of the woman begging in traffic
Shares an expression with mine
I also am begging in traffic
But I don't hold out my naked hand
What I hold out is so naked
It would blind your tourist eyes.

ruined pueblo

Acequia—massacre—you're trying to contain
Something between brackets
Mud bricks or words.
Reach out a hand
And touch the straw
Mixed by slaves.
Citadel is a broken crown
Of rocks
Mycenae—where Agamemnon
Bled into his bath—
Red sea without a god.
When Pecos Pueblo fell
Twenty-seven people, adults and children
Simply picked up and went
Across volcanic fields
To Jemez mountain range
Some tie of language, or sisters-in-law.
Some things you can irrigate
That will never grow—
Grief diminishes
By itself
A salt lake
Shrinking inward,
You can build
Some kind of attempt to hold it—
Find pottery
An amphora painted
With the hero's body
Stretched between Death and Sleep
Or smash it
Like a goblet at a wedding,

*

The groom's foot,
Israelites
Stoned on desert freedom
Behaving as they won't behave again.
The ruined church, fallen convento walls
Some fruit trees
Hibernating in the winter sun
The raven
Flaps a wing just twice a minute
The hummingbird, like the heart,
Beats so much faster.

jack and the beanstalk

The boy hangs upsidedown from the beanstalk—
You don't trust me, but you have no choice
I lie in bed listening to your voice
Come across invisible wires.
After midnight, I go out and plant
Some dangerous seed in hard winter earth:
A green pistachio nut, a dry kidney bean
A piece of my dead husband's bone in ash.
All night a vine will grow
Up to the giant's castle where things
Are much bigger than we are.

Last night I woke at 4 AM
Realized I had fallen in love with you
Again, irrevocably
I had locked you away
A heart that was still beating
In a box of gold with a silver key.
Now the box was open
I could hear it beating
As I set out to climb the beanstalk.

It is Valentine's Day, and hearts are everywhere—
You send me a chocolate heart
In a clear plastic box
But my daughter steals it and eats it.
My friends approve of you
But none of them knows
How hard it is
To climb this beanstalk
Which keeps rising into thin air.

*

I put a robe on over my nightgown
And put on my magic boots
I climb like a rock climber
On the face of Yosemite's El Capitan
I climb like my dead husband
Who once fell asleep in a sycamore tree
I climb like Jack
Whose mother knows he is a fool.
It is easy to find your heart
I slam the lid shut, grab the box, and run.
You don't trust me
Because 23 years ago I forgot
All about your heart.
I come down the beanstalk slowly
Like a toddler down porch steps
Like a yogi entering an asana.
I leave this great weed to stand
In my backyard—
A ladder for angels,
Staircase between heaven and hell,
Shaman's pole,
Like some dreadful Chinese elm
Whose roots will ruin
Thousands of dollars worth of plumbing.
I am ready to return your heart to you.
Or to keep it in my top bureau drawer
With the broken china doll, the condoms,
And my dead husband's sunglasses.
I am almost sorry
You know so much about me
For it will not surprise you that
You have my heart.

eclipse of the moon

As if it were a bonfire, or accident
Neighbors gather on the sidewalk
To watch the total eclipse
Of moon by earth shadow
White disc in and out
Of clouds shaped from a Chinese painting
Then quadrant of clear sky
Moon turning reddish, orange yellow
The kind of color
Dogs howl at.

I wrap myself in a blanket
My daughter climbs on the car
You remember
My black-haired mother
Singing "Total Eclipse"
When we were kids
Even though
It was just a partial eclipse
Of the moon, so long ago.

Penumbra, umbra
Like peri-shadow, or penultimate
Words
The moon charts a course of darkness
Reliable in its change.
Waking many hours later
From lust or fear or the glass of red wine
At four in the morning the white full moon rides high
Above our bed
That's when I realize
I love you both—
The living, and the dead.

andromeda's tears

Star birth—star death
Rings of Saturn—Jupiter's moons
Or Pluto seen as a double planet
You and I circling each other this entire lifetime.
I am a woman with two husbands
One dead, one living
Widow, wife, or a girl
Chained to a rock
Waiting for the dragon.
Certainly you must be the hero Perseus
Who makes a living looking at things indirectly
Skinny and dark-haired, with a narrow face
Your secret is you don't care
About Medusa, that messy lady
With snakes for hair
Your secret is that you love me
Your secret is...
You didn't even know you had a secret.

My mother is a starry w in the sky
Cassiopeia, Queen of Ethiopia, vain, absent.
My secret is that as a child
I loved to pull leaves off bushes
Or shred the white strands of flowers
Called Andromeda's tears
And throw the hard blossoms across the yard
My secret is: I am not really
Chained to the rock
I am free to walk away at any moment.
I want to see what you can do to free me
You have a sword, and something dreadful in that bag
I want to see just how far I can travel

On the kiss of a living man and ten thousand of a dead man.
Blue stars are born in clusters
A galaxy through the telescope
Might be a one-celled creature in a drop of pond water
My tears are free of everything but grief
What infects me is not contagious
I'm standing in the sky on this rock of stars
You can have me. Put out your hand.

comet

A comet above my house
I wear a dead man's coat
I can't see the comet for the haze
Clouds, snow, a waxing moon.

I wear a dead man's coat
A Chinese merchant's of finest wool
Clouds, snow, a waxing moon
The night we said farewell

A Chinese merchant's coat of finest wool
Or the poncho you gave me secondhand
The night we said farewell
For the first time, or the last time

The poncho you gave me secondhand
Wraps around me like a lover
For the first time, or the last time
I watch a movie about astronauts

Wrap around me like a lover
Men in a capsule hurtle towards earth
In a movie about astronauts
I'm crying about something else

Men in a capsule hurtle towards earth
This comet appears once a lifetime
I'm crying about something else
Everyone else has seen it

This comet appears once a lifetime
Above my laundry frozen on the line

Everyone else has seen it
Rising in the quadrant of Arcturus

Beneath my laundry frozen on the line
You say I have a presence
Rising in the quadrant of Arcturus
And the dead I can't speak to

You say: "The comet is a presence"
I can't see for the haze
And the dead I can't speak to
Blaze above my house.

comet hale-bopp

Why is a comet directly over my house?
Why is my husband dead?
Why is a meteor bit of ice and dirt lighting up dawn and dusk
Like a peacock spreading his tail?
This comet looks like a cut-out
Of luminous paper from my daughter's paste the stars on the ceiling kit.
Why can't I glow in the dark?
Why was I never beautiful?
Why have I had so many lovers?
Because I glow in the dark.

The world was created for my sake.
The rabbi suggests I try and live this way.
Comets were created for the comet hunter—
The woman who has discovered the most
Sits on her couch with an afghan, smiling.
There is no thrill like it! she says.
The Japanese comet hunter modestly says:
It is the comet, not I, who should get the credit.
Even the Jewish comet hunter is beaming
As if he had never heard of history.

What does the comet want me to do?
To spend all my money on new summer dresses,
Particularly blue ones with pink flowers.
Why is the oil in my car leaking?
Did I leave the kettle on?
Why are you dead?
Will I get tired of asking this question?
Why do I keep wishing?
Is the telephone for me?
Will my lover kiss me?

Will I get to eat all the black jelly beans
Out of the mix?
Will I find a comet
In an otherwise blank sky of memory
And get to give this comet my last name
Which was probably changed at Ellis Island
As if I were the comet's husband
And it a conventional wife?
Have I ever
Actually seen anything happen?
Will I ever stop saying the words
"My dead husband"?
Has the statute of limitations expired
On being a widow?
Is the check in the envelope?
Will I get to see lava flow?
Will I see a glacier?
Do my cats think?
What's for dinner?
Out of what womb did this comet come?

white sands

I came here to escape my thought
The "I" that puts a lid upon the self
Three hundred square miles of gypsum sand
Might offer white relief:
Albino toad, a scorpion, camouflaged
The color of the rising moon
As earth beneath its sputniks spins
And mortared walls come down.

Berlin, or Carrizozo, New Mexico
Both are places on a map
At Carrizozo's Tastee Freeze
I wonder what she thinks about
The girl who stays and does not leave
Apparently content to serve
Locals and truckers at the crossroads
Of obscure and backcountry routes
Hecate is a crone, a witch
Who rules the criss-crossed left and right
Mammalian upon reptilian brain
As if day overruled black night.

The sky must mark us, live or die
Within each constellation of the round
The rising crab, the setting girl
Space station longing for the ground.
A supernova
In nebula of the crab
Might make a mark
In stone
Carved on Chacoan rock
Beneath a crescent moon

Between two monoliths
Something must rise
In planet orbit east to west
Where is the sight to strike me mute?
I go on talking in the dark.

hunger line

My daughter is studying owls
She tells me: if your owl's
Feathers change color
Feed it more
That is a hunger line
The feathers can break across it

She tells me
How the baby owl
Examines the face of its father
Until it is imprinted
Will let the father feed it

I know nothing about owls
I examine my daughter
For changes that might signal breakage
As she sits on the couch
Holding the photograph of her dead father
He wears a red shirt in the picture
And is glueing a doll's head
Back on to its body

Life is based on the spiral
From lilac embryo
To banana slug DNA
To galaxy
To the heart's left turning golden spiral
To artichoke, to whirlpool, to fiddlehead fern
Spiral unfolds
Also means—things return.

Last night I came home late
My daughter and my lover
Had been out in the dark
Of our shabby neighborhood
Where dogs bark
From equinox to solstice
The new moon hung crescent
Their hands were full
Of dark brown locust pods
That rattled like marimbas
Scimitars full of seeds
Sometimes a father must find
A child not his own
Spiral down
Whose hand is this in mine?
A nautilus shell, a many-chambered molecule.

stones

Stones
Taken from the sea
Lose their lustre,
Still, I cart them back
To my inland
Windowsill
Where two black cats
Bat them down
To dust mice beneath the bed

Stones—dust—water
These are the words of a famous rabbi
I knew a man once
Who spent his life
Cutting out the shapes of river stones
From black Arches paper

My friend collects stones
From all over New Mexico
Pink from the Harding Mine
Green from Pecos
Fairy crosses from up near Taos
One day she decides
To return them all
Life has gone out of these stones
She drives all day
Across the state
Tossing stones out the window

Even what I remember
Of you
Is losing its lustre
Stones—dust—water
Your lost memories
Of earth

more than one buddha

Yesterday, on Canyon Road
I took a turn into a courtyard
The gallery that had been there was gone
More than one Buddha adorned the lawn
Ten or twenty, thirty maybe
Cast from the same mold
Classic cross-legged, eyes cast down
Offerings in the lap of every one
Chrysanthemums, or asters, Mexican sunflowers
Attested that autumn was coming
Strings of prayer flags
Swayed above the garden
The cafe was closed.
Those Buddhas grouped in family arrangements
Remind me, husband, that you are dead
And gone off somewhere without us
Still, all day long
It pleases me to remember
What pleased you—
Umbrellas, teacups, shoes, rain.

green rope

Every day I dance
To the songs you taped
For my fortieth birthday party
And try to read a Rorschach from the dead
In the choice:
Stevie Wonder singing "Don't
You worry 'bout a thing"
A jaunty version of "Bye Bye Love"
Or the original of "Wait a minute
Wait a minute, Mr. Postman"
Which today is the one
That makes me cry.
I jump to the beat
With my green jump rope
As snow melts
On the apricot trees
As new neighbors you will never meet
Move in across the street
Outline their house
In red and green
Of Christmas lights
As a comet appears
Off to the northwest
As the black cats
Bring in the carcass of a mouse
As clover comes up
And your daughter plants primroses.
Before you fell sick
If I'd cling to you in love
You'd say: "Mir, if I died
You'd be married again in six months."
I'd say no, but you were right—

Your outline of ash
Hadn't gone from the world
Before I loved again
If you weren't dead
I'd invite you to the wedding.
Since you died, all night
I climb
The ladder
Between night and day
Like a fire escape
Into the sky
You used to say:
"Mir, if I die
You can run on this one forever...
My dead husband, New Mexico,
My breasts, my dead husband."
You teased me as was your right
First husband of a poet
But you weren't always right—
For now I've used up
All the words
I poured like hard spirits
On your grave.

apocrypha

I lift your fine ashes
Mixed with bone chips
To my forehead—
Then pour them
Into the open grave
Through a funnel of red foil paper.

A dog
Interrupts the ceremony
Might drink water from the basin
Used to wash the gravestone
As if it were a newborn
Or a corpse.

You're not here—
That much is obvious
By the pot of white orchids
Piñon and spruce
Rustling in the spring wind

A neat trick
To put the Dharmakaya
Into a boulder
Good work
If you can get it

Good-bye to you
I bow
To everything I loved

prehistory

Six years after
Her husband's death
The paleontologist
Finds footprints
Preserved in volcanic ash:
Two adults and a small one
Walking upright.

History is malleable—
Widow
Of a faithless husband
Solitary woman
Alone in rift country.
Her most important
Discovery:
That we have been walking
So much longer
Than we'd imagined.

a lockless key

after a Massimo Bartolini Installation, 1997

Some things are beautiful with the life leached out—
Atlantic tideline of moonshells, shark cartilege, those black
Egg sacs of skates
That until puberty I thought
Were four-legged, headless sea creatures in their own right
Odd collections of paperbacks warping in the sea air
Pages buckling like fault-lines
A life spent in rented houses
Houses with two white chipped teacups in each cupboard
Piles of children's games
Missing all the dice
Nests of mice beneath sofa cushions.
And the ring of keys
Each with its forgotten use
The missing lock
To somewhere else.

I once saw a houseguest
A beautiful woman with six months left to live
Read French *Vogue*
At the time I thought it
A poor choice—
Now I understand.

The yellow wall recedes from my touch.
At first I didn't see
The one-holed constellation in the roof
One star alone
Can make no pattern—
Bear, girl chained to a rock, queen, or lion.
Last night I wasn't exactly pleased
To see you run after

The city bus in the dream
It must have been San Francisco
Because you were so young in your long beard
You banged on the window
Said, "I just want to give you a hug
Before I die."
I had a motto:
Never write about your dreams,
Dreams are a different
Kind of condensed milk
In a red and silver can
That should only be drunk
In black coffee
In the dark.

Only now do I notice
Stars shining
On the yellow kitchen table
Moving from the southern hemisphere
Into something unrecognizable
My daughter demands
A grown-up to lift down
First a gold crown, then a witch's hat
From the high shelf
I don't recognize myself in the mirror
My own shoes frighten me
Ordinary household appliances
Are marked, as we are
By the course of stars
The burns on the breakfast toast
Are simply stars
Not yet born.

about the author

Miriam Sagan is author of more than a dozen books of poetry, fiction, and nonfiction. She has held residency grants at Yaddo and MacDowell and is the recipient of a grant from the Barbara Deming Foundation and a Border Regional Library Association Award.

Ahsahta Press

New Series

LANCE PHILLIPS, *Corpus Socius*

Modern and Contemporary Poetry of the American West

This book is set in Apollo type with Futura titles
by Ahsahta Press at Boise State University
and manufactured on acid-free paper
by the Boise State University Print Shop,
Boise, Idaho.

AHSAHTA PRESS
2002

JANET HOLMES, DIRECTOR

CAROLYN FRITSCHLE   JOSH KENNEDY

FARGO KESEY   RUSSELL KING

SHANNON MAHONEY   WILLIAM GUY MILLER

MAURA PAYNE   MATT REITER

ANTHONY HADLEY, INTERN